Old HANDSWORTH, LOZELLS, BIRCHFIELD &

by

Eric Armstrong

NO. 1087B.

Council House. Handsworth.

This fine redbrick seat of local government, built during the late 1870s, also housed a public library and art school. The sheep crossing the road suggest either an escape from a vehicle, or a field or two not far away. *4 March 1938. Went to library. X there. Still smiles and looks. Must get to know X.* (An ambition never realised. X was a pretty assistant!)

© Eric Armstrong 1999
First published in the United Kingdom, 1999,
by Stenlake Publishing, Ochiltree Sawmill, The Lade,
Ochiltree, Ayrshire, KA18 2NX
Telephone / Fax: 01290 423114

ISBN 1 84033 075 9

FURTHER READING

The books listed below were used by the author during his research. None of them are available from Stenlake Publishing. Those interested in finding out more are advised to contact their local bookshop or reference library.

Handsworth Remembered, Vincent J. Price, Brewin Books, 1992.

Birmingham on Old Postcards, John Marks; Vol. 1, 1982; Vol. 2, 1983; Vol. 3, 1990; Reflections of a Bygone Age.

The Dream Palaces of Birmingham, Chris & Rosemary Clegg, published by the authors, 1983.

The Aston Villa Story, Ian Johnson, Arthur Baker Ltd., 1981.

Aston Villa, A Portrait in Old Picture Postcards, Derrick Spinks, S.B. Publications, 1991.

Growing Up and Ducking Down, Eric Armstrong, Minerva Press, 1997. (Available from bookshops priced £6.99. Please quote ISBN 1 86106 275 3.)

In the early years of this century, extensive areas of Handsworth were regarded as 'highly desirable residential'. The message on this card reads: '17 Livingstone Road - March 1908 to end of May 1909'. At the time many families employed a maid, and the message probably refers to the person in the picture's period of service at this house.

During the 1930s the Regal was one of Birmingham's finest cinemas. Opened in 1929 with a 'talkies' programme, it could seat over 2,000 film fans, although I wonder how many went to see 'Four Men and a Prayer'. *6 May 1939. Saw Margaret at night, went to the Regal, 'The Citadel', 1/3 seats. Celebrating.* (Success at the school sports that afternoon. Being a Saturday evening and a fine film, the cinema was packed.)

NEW INNS, HANDSWORTH.

G.7945.

Two major landmarks on Holyhead Road. The Albion cinema opened in 1916 and was later enlarged to appear as it does in the photograph. The M&B (Mitchells and Butlers brewery) New Inns Hotel was Handsworth's premier location for a 'bit of a do'. M&B began brewing for Brummagem and Black Country thirsts in 1879.

Banqueting Room and Ball Room at New Inns Hotel Holyhead Rd Handsworth

All descriptions of social functions catered for.

A convivial place to be when full. According to a recent publicity brochure about Sandwell, an area adjoining Handsworth, 'the [Mitchells and Butlers] brewery has recently undergone an award winning major redevelopment and restoration programme costing £11.5m but still retains original coppers and mash tuns'. Organised tours are available.

A typical Soho Road scene. The clock tower of the Council House is visible in the distance. Competing Woolworths and Peacocks stores are in evidence, with a branch of the shoe shop Freeman Hardy Willis standing to the right of Woolies.

The technical school, located in Golds Hill Road. The road runs parallel to a section of Soho Road and is only a short distance from Soho Avenue, where Soho House, home of Matthew Boulton, the industrialist colleague of Watt and Murdock, has recently been restored. The school was built at a cost of £11,500 and opened in 1897.

King Edward's Grammar School for Girls (Handsworth) is one of Birmingham's most prestigious schools, and celebrated its centenary in 1983. *30 August 1939. Had to take message to Rose Hill Road School* (the school in the picture). *Girls in hall. Sounded like a cage of parrots.* (Small wonder! Pre-evacuation tension and excitement were in the air.)

Industrious teachers in the staff room at King Edward's. Were they marking homework, or was it all a pose for the photographer? 'Putting up one's hair' seems to have been fashionable at the time. Parquet flooring, flowers on the tables and what might be a telephone on the middle pillar suggest that this is a cultured and well-run school.

This fine church stands at the crossroads of Birchfield Road with Heathfield Road and Trinity Road. Trinity Road, to the right of the bollards, leads to an arena of lay 'worship', Villa Park, long the home of Aston Villa FC. *26 August 1939. Went to the Villa match . . . beat Middlesborough 2-0. Very good game. Nobody suffering from crisitis. First thing men did at the match when they bought evening papers was to look at the racing results on the back page. Eight days later Britain was at war with Germany.* ('Crisitis' - a word invented by the sixteen-year-old diarist to summarise the tensions experienced by British people on the brink of war.)

Hamstead Road Baptist Church was built in the early 1880s at a cost of £10,000 with seating for up to 800 worshippers. The horse-drawn vehicle is turning into Villa Road in the direction of Soho Road. The card is postmarked 1912.

Villa Road, Handsworth.

The bustling shopping section of Villa Road. Behind the tram stands one of Handsworth's best-known pubs, the Villa Cross Hotel. For a period, the pub's landlord was a former Aston Villa player. FRANKLIN, and presumably POOLE, with their advert on the gable end might be selling kippers or slippers, but are most likely a family draper's. The postcard, depicting a peaceful everyday scene, was written on 7 August 1918 with the First World War still raging in France.

Lozells Road, another busy shopping area. Another branch of Woolies ('nothing over 6d') did a brisk business in this area in the 1930s. The corner shop, right, by Berners Street, gives much prominence to its wines and spirits trade. *12 February 1938. Bought 'Air Trails' from Woolworth's Lozells at night. 3d.* (Air Trails was an aviation magazine.)

LOZELLS ST MAY FESTIVAL 1928

Gym-slips galore! During the 1920s, dancing round the maypole was a common feature of infant/junior school life - usually unpopular with the boys and certainly so with the compiler.

13

Lozells Picture House, one of Birmingham's oldest cinemas, opened in 1911 and was rebuilt in 1922. A Wurlitzer organ was installed in 1927 on which the popular Frank Newman played. Newman was a highly regarded cinema organist, well-known during the 1930s for his regular radio broadcasts. The cinema was destroyed during a 1942 air raid.

14

Six Ways, a busy and well-known traffic hub with tram routes leading to Witton, Aston, Birmingham city centre, Lozells, and Perry Barr. What looks like a three-wheeled car is heading towards Perry Barr. Could it be a Morgan? The rather imposing building on the left-hand corner is a branch of The London City and Midland Bank.

Odeon, Perry Barr.

Dating from 1930, this was the first Odeon cinema to be opened in Britain. It marked the beginning of Oscar Deutsch's Odeon circuit, which at one time numbered nearly 300 cinemas throughout the country. In view of a subsequent event when a UXB (unexploded bomb) was lodged under the cinema's foundations, the title of the supporting film, 'Dangerous Age' was prophetic. This card was posted on 3 September 1937. *21 August 1938. Went to see 'King Kong' at the Odeon. Talk about tough. I'll say. 26 October 1940. 'Pinocchio', a wonderful production. Galaxy of colours, makes you realise that after all there is something beautiful and creative in the world. Huge glowing fire, engines tearing to town. Bombs quite close again. Stap me.*

PERRY BARR

63

The lady in the light-coloured hat is walking past the small but homely Birchfield Picture House, which opened in 1912. The card is postmarked 1918. Adjacent to the cinema is the public library. Across the way, the Ansell's slogan can readily be completed to read 'Ansell's Aston Ales'. The 'Birchies' and the Odeon were only five minutes walk apart. *31 January 1939. Went with Margaret to see Dracula and Frankenstein. Not particularly horrifying but thrilling all the same. Had a great time. Packed house.* Perry Barr, like Handsworth, was originally part of Staffordshire. The area was incorporated into Birmingham in 1928.

17

Perry Barr tram terminus. The No. 6 tram ran from this point to Birmingham city centre. A well-known local pub, The Crown and Cushion, stands at the left-hand corner. To the right (out of shot) Aston Lane leads to Witton and Villa Park. Wellington Road leads off to the left. Aston Villa's first 'real' ground (where gate money of 3d was charged) was situated in Wellington Road just a few minutes walk from an earlier Crown and Cushion, which from 1876 to 1897 served as the club's 'headquarters'. This photograph was taken in March 1938.

Reading left to right, the placards outside the corner shop proclaim: Xmas Gift Books For Your Children; Built Staircase in Xmas Cracker (a puzzle that one!); Mystery of Injured Cyclist in Church; Cup Tie Coupons for Xmas Cash; Will There be Another War? The photograph was probably taken in December 1938. This corner shop sold Meccano, and the advertising sign can just be made out in the side window above the HA of Handsworth. The shop stood at the corner of Oxhill and Windermere Roads.

CHURCH LANE HANDSWORTH

Rather grander housing was - and is - to be found in Church Lane, as befits a road adjoining Handsworth Wood, an area long regarded as the posh part of Handsworth. The compiler's grandfather, who could neither read nor write, worked as a jobbing gardener for some of Handsworth Wood's residents during the 1930s.

Much older cottages, also in Church Lane, indicative of an earlier semi-rural Handsworth. These cottages, photographed at various times of the year, feature on many postcards. *23 November 1940. Felt like something the cat had dragged in at work this morning. Had to make detours. Bombs Church Lane, Oxhill Road, Island Road. Terrible damage. No water or gas.*

WELLINGTON RD. HANDSWORTH

From Perry Barr, Wellington Road runs virtually due west to the start of Church Lane. This photograph, taken near the corner of Howard Road, shows typical Handsworth residential property.

Sandwell Road, on the approach to one of Handsworth's boundaries. This continues into Island Road, followed by Holyhead Road, and Birmingham Road which leads westwards to West Bromwich and the Black Country.

Although not visible in the picture, the title of this postcard is 'Handsworth, The Grove'. The Grove Pub, on the left, is an Ansell's house dating back to 1891. The stretch of dual carriageway, albeit short, in Grove Lane, was unusual in older suburbia dating from before the Second World War. The card was posted in August 1927.

Situated in Grove Lane and built in 1907 at a cost of £21,500, these baths were a boon to swimmers - and bathers who had no bath at home (many houses had no bath). There were 1st and 2nd class swimming facilities, as well as Turkish and private baths. The swimming baths were much used by schools. *14 April 1938. Went to Grove Lane Baths with Allan, 2nd Class. 3d. 18 September 1938. (Margaret) looks a treat in a bathing costume - oh boy!*

Handsworth. Grove Lane Schools. Aho Series 130

The council school, dating from 1903, stands in the foreground with Dawson Road leading off to the right beyond it. Handsworth Grammar School is in the distance. The tramlines are veering left towards Soho Road; the left turning in the foreground leads into Mostyn Road.

G.7944.

GRAMMAR SCHOOL, HANDSWORTH.

Handsworth Grammar School for Boys, in Grove Lane, was founded by the Bridge Trust in 1862. Places were (and still are) keenly sought-after. This was the school attended by the author between 1934 and 1940 (from 1939 to 1940 the school was evacuated from Birmingham to Stroud in the Cotswolds). The school badge still bears a representation of the Zig Zag bridge, Perry Barr (see page 47), and of the Staffordshire knot. Both symbols are indicative of Handsworth's historic association with Staffordshire.

The Hollygate Cafe, Handsworth. Very occasionally, and only in the summer heat, a stop would be made here for a ginger beer when walking home from school. The cafe was situated in Holly Road, close to one of the main entrances to Handsworth Park.

Handsworth. Park Bowling Green. Ana Series 157.

Handsworth Park was opened in 1887 to commemorate Queen Victoria's Jubilee, and was first known as Victoria Park. For many Brummies it was the city's most prestigious park, well-known as the venue for major flower shows, Boy Scouts' rallies, galas and other events. *15 July 1939. Eddie and I went to the ARP* (air-raid precautions) *Rally in Handsworth Park. Good march-past. Blazing house put out. Artillery and anti-aircraft guns in action.* The house, of course, was a mock-up.

BANDSTAND, HANDSWORTH PARK, HANDSWORTH. G.7950

The open area behind and to the right of the bandstand was known as the cricket pitch. Rallies and march-pasts were held there, with tents and marquees erected on the pitch and the sloping grassland in the distance. *3 May 1938. Date for tomorrow night by bandstand.* (The date was kept, but Muriel was held to be *'very fast'*!)

THE BOATHOUSE VICTORIA PARK, HANDSWORTH. D

A popular boating lake. During the very severe winter weather of 1940, the boathouse roof collapsed under the weight of snow. The dark objects hanging on the railings are thought to be boat seating cushions. *3 April 1940. First time I have had a skiff out. Managed quite well, but you certainly have to be careful and sit tight.* (Evacuee back home from Stroud for Easter break).

HANDSWORTH PARK LODGE
HAMSTEAD RD.

An imposing park lodge and impressive wrought iron gates, standing open here and allowing a view of fields where 1930s semis were later built.

CROMPTON RD. HANDSWORTH

Back home to Crompton Road, where the compiler was born (although not in this particular part of the street). The horse-drawn van bears the legend 'Baker and Confectioner, 99 Birchfield Road'. Further down the road is an open, low-floored cart carrying the milkman's churns. The card is postmarked 1915, but the road seemed much the same some 20 years later.

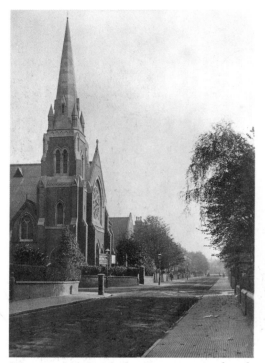

WESTMINSTER RD. HANDSWORTH

Westminster Road Congregational Church was built in 1882, and promoted a very active social club on its premises. This offered snooker, table tennis, beetle drives, and Saturday night dances with 78 rpm records played on the radiogram. Livingstone Road runs to the left of the pillar box with Putney Road opposite. Note the hard-wearing, wavy 'blue brick' type pavement. *20 August 1939. Worst preacher I have ever heard. Thunderstorm afterwards. 3 September 1939* (the day war broke out). *Umpteen barrage balloons in the sky. Went to church in the afternoon and at night.*

12 December 1940. Terrific bang . . . room seemed to shake and close in on me. Blew one of the front windows out. Dashed up to Westminster and Wellington Roads (with Mother) *to see if everyone was all right* ('everyone' being the relations). *Just to the right of the lamp-post, where the pavement slopes to the road, a car stood with its windows open. For a few minutes this served as an air-raid shelter as mother and son shoved heads and shoulders into its interior. This ludicrous sight was perhaps only seen by a German bomb aimer!* The madcap scamper through falling shrapnel from British ack-ack guns had begun in Hutton Road, the entrance to which is in the middle distance on the right.

HEATHFIELD RD.
HANDSWORTH

Among the group of shops with their awnings serving as sunshades there was an 'Aladdin's cave', a newsagent's-cum-toy-fair which stocked, amongst many other things, Bowman stationary steam engines. These could be used to drive models made from Meccano. By cutting back on sweets and comics over a period of months, threepenny bits and tanners were put into an Aladdin's Christmas Club fund and eventually the magical total of fourteen shillings and sixpence was reached. A Bowman was mine!

35

BREAD MAKING PLANT
AT GEORGE BAINES'
MODEL BAKERY.

This is one of a series of postcards presumably produced by Baines' for promotional purposes. Others illustrate the different processes involved in the baking of bread. The images suggest that this bakery used state-of-the-art technology and maintained the highest standards of food hygiene, hence perhaps the description 'model bakery'. When bread was being baked this was a wonderfully fragrant factory to saunter past, on the way to or from shopping 'on the Lozells'. The bakery was located in Finch Road.

Heathfield Road. In 1874, near a gas light in Heathfield Road (an indirect tribute to Scottish inventor William Murdock - see page 43), several young cricketers decided to play football during the non-cricketing months. This is accepted as the beginnings of what became Aston Villa FC.

'Under the clock at Bendall's corner' was a popular meeting place for, among others, schoolboy footballers who were playing away from their home pitch that Saturday. Villa Cross pub can be seen in the distance.

Hamstead Road, with one of the main entrances to Handsworth Park at the bottom of the hill on the left-hand side. The top of the tower of St Mary's church can just be seen among the trees.

The Handsworth parish church of St Mary's, which dates back to the twelfth century, has long been associated with three of Birmingham's most famous sons, allowing that two of them were adopted, having been born in Scotland. The names of James Watt, William Murdock and Matthew Boulton (born in Birmingham) are inseparably linked with Handsworth and the Soho Engineering Works. James Watt died at Heathfield Hall in 1819 and the centenary of his death was commemorated by, among many other things, a set of postcards (see pages 42 and 43). When raising money during the 1980s for church repairs the fund organisers justifiably claimed that the church constituted the ' "Westminster Abbey" of the Industrial Revolution'. Boulton, Watt and Murdock are all buried in the vaults of St Mary's.

James Watt's garret workshop at his home, Heathfield Hall. After the demolition of the house *c.*1924, a reconstruction of the workshop was built within the Science Museum in London. Some of the original floorboards were used for this purpose and through the glass in the original window frame visitors can look into the workshop as it was left at the time of Watt's death. The busts on the workbench serve as a reminder that Watt invented two machines for the copying of sculptures. The room contains more than 6,000 objects.

James Watt (1736-1819), was born in Greenock. After learning the trade, he became Glasgow University's mathematical instrument maker, holding the post from 1757 to 1763. He was employed on various canal, river and harbour surveys in Scotland. Early in his career Watt became interested in steam power and rapidly developed ideas to improve the efficiency of the then prevailing Newcomen steam engine. In 1774 he formed a partnership with Matthew Boulton of Soho, near Birmingham, and the manufacture of the new Watt's steam engine was begun at the Soho Engineering Works. Watt continued to invent other engineering devices including a letter copying press. A unit of power, the watt, was named after him.

James Watt Centenary Commemoration Birmingham, 1919.

SUN & PLANET ENGINE supplied by BOULTON AND WATT in 1797 to John Maud of London.

James Watt Centenary Commemoration, BIRMINGHAM, 1919.

Statue in Memorial Chapel, in Handsworth Church
by Chantrey.

Born in Birmingham the son of a silver stamper, Matthew Boulton (1728-1809) expanded the family business with the building of the engineering works in Soho, opened in 1762. As well as manufacturing Watt's steam engines, the firm also improved coining machinery and a Boulton press remained in use at the Mint until 1882. The Lunar Society, a group of fourteen eminent scientists, engineers and scholars met monthly at Boulton's home, Soho House. As well as Watt and Boulton (himself an FRS), the group included Dr Joseph Priestley (chemist) Dr Erasmus Darwin (physician, botanist and grandfather of Charles Darwin) and Josiah Wedgwood (potter). Soho House has recently been restored to its original elegance.

WILLIAM MURDOCH,
INVENTOR OF GAS LIGHTING. Born, Bello Mill, Lugar, 1745.
Died, Sycamore House, Handsworth, Birmingham, 1839.

HEATHFIELD HALL
The home of James Watt.

William Murdock (1754-1839 (the date 1745 on the card is wrong)) was born in Ayrshire. After working with his millwright father he joined Boulton and Watt in Birmingham, who sent him to Cornwall to build mining engines. He made a number of engineering innovations including improvements to Watt's engine. While in Redruth he began to distil coal gas, carrying out a number of experiments to establish what it could be used for. In 1803 the Soho premises became gas lit, and it is as the father of gas lighting that Murdock will be best remembered.

Wood Lane.
Handsworth.

A semi-rural scene of Handsworth past. Eventually, neat semi-detached houses were built on either side of the lane. At the road's lower end elements of the countryside remain in the form of a wooded frontage to a working men's social club and adjacent allotments. By building a service road parallel to the stretch of lane shown, it became possible to retain part of the hedgerow.

Old cottages at the higher end of Wood Lane at the junction with Butler's Road. The sender of the card has written: 'It's a very nice place to be 'with an armful of girl in the twi twilight'. Hope you have got over missing your supper beer.' 'In the twi twilight' was a snatch from a popular music hall song. The card is postmarked August 1910.

HANDSWORTH COLLEGE.

Handsworth College, located in Friary Road. Built at a cost of £40,000 and set in grounds of 23 acres, this Wesleyan Theological College for would-be Methodist ministers was opened in 1881. 'The college is a fine place. I have a study & bedroom to myself. There are 68 of us in residence. The 5 hours from 9 a.m. to 2 p.m. are occupied in attending lectures given by the tutors; the afternoon is spent in recreation - from 2:45 to 5:15 & the evening study.' (The postcard was written in 1912.)

HOLLOWAY.

HANDSWORTH

Sport in Handsworth Wood during summer 1910. The cricket match between 'These and Those', played on 'Rugby Football ground Handsworth Wood Road', was presumably a light-hearted affair (the quotations are from the back of the card).

2410 THE ZIG ZAG BRIDGE, PERRY BARR

Moving north-east to the Perry Barr outskirts of Handsworth Wood and the much photographed Zig Zag bridge. Rapid and vast increases in motorised traffic, including the introduction of Corporation buses, subsequently made it necessary to build a modern bridge parallel to the Zig Zag bridge across the murky waters of the River Tame.

ENTRANCE TO PARK, PERRY BARR.

This park, just north of the Zig Zag bridge, became the home of the famous athletics club, The Birchfield Harriers, during the post World War II era. *12 September 1938. Went to Perry Park. Got to know 2 very nice girls. Amy. Margaret.* (The great romance had begun!) *12 August 1939. Watched the terriers (Territorial Army) in camp in Perry Park.* The countdown to war had started.

48